This Motherloving Life

Priya Mohanty

BookLeaf
Publishing

Presentation by *BookLeaf Publishing*

Web: www.bookleafpub.com

E-mail: info@bookleafpub.com

ISBN: 9789357615358

First edition 2022

*To my beautiful daughters who chose me to
be their Mama*

*To my husband - my partner in this
motherloving life*

ACKNOWLEDGEMENT

To my dad for the amazing cover art

The Day She Was Born

The day she was born
My heart swelled in size
Love and light? Yes, yes of course..
But also - I feel something else arise.

Something tangled and knotty
Throwing shadows on my joy
A sudden vulnerability
And as much I try
I cannot put it aside.

I want so much for her
I want the sunshine, rainbows and love
I'd offer her the world
But it doesn't seem enough
Because the world isn't full
Of sunshine and rainbows
Sometimes it's gloomy
Quite often it's cold.

But here is what I wish for her-
To not inherit my burdens
That cross is mine to bear
The best I can do is to arm her
For the world as it is

To find the joy and the laughter
Because yes - they do exist.

There is much to unlearn
There is much to change
This cycle needs breaking
New ways to be claimed
I am ready and yet I'm not
But that's ok…..
I'm giving it my best shot.

Retinol

I should have used retinol
And sunscreen.
Definitely sunscreen
Oh! and Vitamin C Serum
To get that perpetually sun kissed glow
To get those fine lines to slow.
When does the fight to fight the inevitable
begin?
To slow times march and the clocks rhythm
Since I was born, my body and face
Have been lathered and slathered
In a fools attempts to win this race
'Don't frown, you'll get those lines'
'You'll get a tan! Don't step in the sunshine'
But what's so wrong with fine lines and a tan?
Nothing apparently, if you are a man.

The Push

'She pushed a boy in class today'
Her teacher told me
'Did you?' I ask to see what she has to say
She nods silently.
'Hands are not for pushing. We know that , don't
we?'
I gently prod further
'What happened? How do you feel?'
She looks at me with her sweet innocent eyes
'He grabbed my hand in a way I didn't like'
I suppress a smile and wait to see what she says
'So I pushed him and asked him to give me
some space'
I resist the urge to cheer her on
And say 'That's fine but to use our hands is
wrong'
I encourage her to use her words instead
And pranayam breaths to calm her head.
But as a mother I do feel a surge of pride
That she can move through the world and
demand her space
In a manspreading world that will force her to
hide
I hope she feels ready to always claim her place.

Charmed Life

I have dreams of a life extraordinary
To live a life full of wondrous stories
Follow the path the world least expects
With head held high and stony grit
Achieve renown and respect
In a field chosen as my heart sees fit.

Learn an obscure language or two
Make a movie and publish a book
Learn to cook from all the nonnas and dadis
Pasta from scratch and biriyani Hyderabadi
Travel the length and breadth of this earth
See what ethereal sights we can unearth.

Grow my own veggies and fruits
And then cook up my very own loot
Make the best chocolate brownies ever
With the most decadent heavenly flavor
That will always remind my children of home
Like a warm hug when they are alone
Make every game and wipe every tear
So I can win 'Mommy of the year'.

I want to do it all and I want to do it now

But as time marches on, my ambitions they
transform
Giving myself the time my patience now allows
Not worry about where I'm going or where I
come from
No - I haven't given up on my dreams
I still visit them sometimes
But when I focus on the here and now it seems
That I am already living a really charmed life.

Beautiful Me

'You look beautiful, mommy' she says
Disrupting my intent gaze in the mirror
'What did you say?' - I ask her
'You look beautiful' she repeats
Words I meet with incredulity,
I look at myself
Strawberry skin on legs and arms
Tiger belly stripes and c section scar
Saggy breasts and wobbly thighs
A jiggling mass of cellulite
All exposed in the unforgiving light,
If my body belonged to some one else
I'd probably treat it with more respect
But when it comes to myself and me
I seem to find every flaw and folly.
I look at my face
With its crags and crevices
Pitted grooves and blemishes
Fine lines I always meant to moisturize
Dark circles I can't seem to hide,
I look at her
Her bright beautiful eyes and button nose
Her dazzling smile and soft finger curls
I wish she could see herself through my eyes
But I also wish I could see myself through hers.

The way to do that is stupidly simple
It's to stop obsessing every fold and pimple
Knowing she is watching and taking her cue
from me
Now is the time to set the self hate free
And start to love myself and beautiful me.

Adverbs

'Why did you lock it?' He asks
Jiggling the handle of the car door
I unlock them so he can get in
'To keep myself safe, of course'
It seems obvious to me, but not him.
Must be nice to walk through the world
And not worry about the little things
Being on red high alert perpetually
Looking over your shoulder constantly
Walking in the dark carefully
All these adverbs ingrained in us
That's just how it is to be a woman
This behavior learned with no fuss
Laughably normal. Furiously common.
We've learnt the ways to keep us safe
The best ways to hold the car keys in your hand
Because clearly it's all about how WE behave
The only one beyond reproach is the man.

Rest

That familiar pang of unsettling guilt
Defines my worth and existence,
As if my life and everything I built
Is reigned in by this invisible fence
Of expectations of hustle culture,
Where the idea of rest is one to deplore,
And the indulgence of simple pleasures
Is too much for us to explore.

A bizarre pride in the scarcity of time,
We wear it as a badge of honor,
Just step back and take a moment to find
A moment of serenity in a calming corner.

There is a tenderness in the slowing down
Treating each moment with reverence,
There is a wide expanse to be found
If we were to go beyond that self made fence.

In a world that chooses to define our worth
By output and productivity,
The very act of rest is revolt
Ushering endless possibilities.

DMER

'It's the best feeling in the world'
Is what they all said,
But when I feed my little girl
All I feel is a pitted dread
That rush of oxytocin to help bond with my
child?
With bated breath I wait for a while
Instead what I notice and find
Like clockwork every single time
A pit in my stomach and a sinking heart
Every time my let down starts
The internet reliably has a name for it
Dysphoric Milk Ejection Reflex
As puzzled as I am, my doctors know even less.
Let down by my let down,
I can see the irony here
But in the midst of this here's what I found -
That I shouldn't have had to fear
A lack of love, attachment or bond
Because breast or not- my heart it grew
And made me capable of a love I never knew.
So I sit here now attached to tubes and pump
Massaging away a stubborn lump
Knowing fully well that fed is best
I can lay my anxiety to rest.

The Little Girl

It's a big empty room in a big empty house,
The silence bubbles over and wraps itself
around.
My pigtails dangle, my little hands grasp empty
air,
My feet threaten to betray as I stumble down the
stairs.

These blindfolds – they itch; I try and take a
peek,
All I see are slivers and shadows; forming
pictures incomplete.
A knock on the knee, a stub on my toe, help me
find my way,
Am I really hearing voices? They mock and lead
me astray.

I stumble, I waver, I crawl and I fall,
Bruises and blisters, scabs now grown old,
Silly little me takes a while to realize,
All I have to do is take those blindfolds off my
eyes.

Overwhelmed with new light, awash with the
glow,

My senses adjust; the newness takes ahold.
My eyes see a picture that my mind cannot
grasp,
Of a woman, old and wizened, with a sash in her
clasp.
I look around the room and here is what I see,
Dust settled on grand ideas, cobwebs on my
dreams,
And then it finally dawns – that woman is me.

Two Worlds

I'm stuck between two worlds
In a limbo of a kind
Tethered to the past by one
The other my future binds

One the place of birth
That made me who I am
Family & friends who know me well
Forever tie me to this land

The other helped me open up
To a life different and new
Embrace change and everything with it
Gave my life a fresh view

This question I now ponder
Where do I belong?
Not completely part of one or other
And yet neither feel wrong

I live in a quandary
Till I face the honest truth
Where once I had one home
I now have two

New Song

Riding through the mist, looking for a song
Forces blurring, feelings churning
Memories not so strong

Anathema to myself, for reasons I can't define
At the crossroads, winding through looking for
some sign

Need a word, need a tune, to string a melody in
time
Build the faith, find the truth, dedicated to the
shrine

Dredging up a dulcet tone, encased in memory
deep
Ring of laughter, love & life and promises to
keep

Let the past pave the way, for things yet to come
An old tune to play anew, the euphony to strum

Home

Family, friends, food & fun
Scorching heat, cold winter sun
Festivals that bring everyone together
Laughter, lights and color through every weather
Enveloped in a cocoon of love and care
So much to give, so much to share
A place where I can be me
No pretensions, no guile for others to see
In moments waking and asleep I stray
Back to the place where my heart truly roams
Home is where the heart is, they say
But I left my heart back at home

Rainy Days

Rainy days take me back in time
Vada pau at a stall in Mumbai
Hot pakoras and garam cutting chai
That rain scented earth smell
Infusing the air
Green becoming greener
New life everywhere

Gargantuan waves
Crashing down the rocks
As purposeful adults take their walk
Gleeful children with less purpose
Mocking the mighty wave
And in puddles, playing hopscotch.

Me buried under a blanket
A good book and hot chai
Snuggled in the cosiness
Watching the world go by

I've travelled miles away
And look! How I have grown!
Time may have passed but even today
Rainy days make me miss home.

Good Cry

'Don't cry' we were always told
Sometimes a gentle urge, sometimes an
impatient command
As if our tears were a personal affront
Instead of just our bodies emotional sweat
Keeping those big feelings on a perpetual hold
With the hope that you will soon forget
The cause and root, the how and why
Bury any hope of introspection
With the sole aim being to stifle any cry
'Good girls don't cry' was the common refrain
And so we grew up not knowing why
Our emotions we struggle to tame
And the toxic buildup
Of feelings pent up
Poisons us slowly as it courses through
Our synapses
Fundamentally altering our brain
Something needs to change, I recognize
But sometimes it feels too late
My brains plasticity has lost its elasticity
To find a way to emotional regulate
So now I teach my daughters
'Crying is good. It's ok to cry'
Sweat it out. Let it out.

Deep breaths. Get a hug. Read a book. Maybe
even shout.
Feel all your feelings. Validate. Regulate.
The goal isn't to get them to stop feeling
It's to give them the tools to do their own
healing
The hardest part of this parenting gig
Is the unlearning. Relearning. Reparenting.
Teaching while learning.
It's hard to learn when I'm supposed to be
modeling
But I've been working hard and I've picked up a
few new skills
So I take my deep breaths and force my mind to
be still
It's okay to be overwhelmed, I'll give it another
try
And maybe I'll even let myself cry.

Motherloving life

Unkempt hair, unslept eyes
A forsaken cup of coffee
The luxury of sleeping in
Seems like a distant memory,
Constant claims on time and attention
clamors of simultaneous cries,
A deluge of feelings threaten to flood
Even as I patiently answer every 'But why?'
In my head is the constant reminder
'It's me and not her'
She's just being a toddler,
Every question and every tantrum
Every meltdown and every conundrum
Is pivotal in their moulding,
As hard as it is for me it's even harder for them.
Meet every question with an answer
And applaud their intellectual curiosity,
Meet every tantrum with empathy
Breathe through the meltdowns
Because they are teaching moments too,
What you model for them will be reflected back
to you
And if you're figuring it out, they will figure it
out with you
And when they face a conundrum

Give them space to find a way through.
Try your best and know that with every measure
Of love and patience you give them, you become
their inner voice - no pressure!
It isn't easy - this mother-loving life,
But you will find to your surprise
That you have more patience than you know
This inexorable love will help you dig deep
And with it your heart and you will grow.
Then one day they will have asked a 'but why?'
For the very last time
And there are no more inexplicable tears
No placating their outsized fears,
Your coffee no longer sits cold, undergoing
repeated trips to the microwave,
And then it will be time to step back and steer
clear
Knowing you've done your best to keep them
safe
And let them be who they need to be
And hard as it will be, we let them free.

Failure to fail

'It probably won't be great' I say
Preempting my failure,
Never even giving myself a chance
Even before I've started I've said I can't,
'It's really not my best work' I tell people
Not sure who I'm fooling with this pretense of
modesty
So thinly veiled, the attempt seems feeble
Sometimes honesty is the best policy.
Really those words are more for me than you
Why expect much from me and face
disappointment
So much better to prepare my heart
And leave no room for resentment .
It's hard to be resentful towards yourself
Disappointed in yourself
Can't leave the room, can't walk away
Wouldn't want those icky feelings to stay.
So expect less
Don't make a mess
Honestly, that's the best play.
When you grow up believing failure is not an
option
Every misstep feels disproportionally like the
end

But the real failure is the lack of action
The fear that stops you from any attempt,
Accepting defeat even before you start
Failing is good, failing is key, embrace
everything it entails
Give failure a chance, fail at everything, fail at it
hard
The only real failure is the failure to fail.

Roots

When do you grow your roots?
When do you find home?
As a child perhaps
Nurtured by family
Cocooned in safety
Free to take a stumble and fall
A helping hand to help you stand tall.
Maybe in your teens
When the whole world unfurls
A mulchy mix of hormones and emotions swirl
And the rich soil of knowledge and learning
And the warmth of friendship and young
yearning
Give new shoots to your dimension
And imbues you with fresh motivation.
Is it when you find your calling?
Call it purpose or destiny
It's what you're meant to be,
Or how about when your bear your offshoots of
offspring
And you find yourself transformed by a new
stirring,
A way to perpetuate to propagate
And hope they carry the best do your traits.
Where do you grow your roots?

In a time or place or person?
When the labor of all this growth bears fruit
And all things are said and done
Here is what you need to know
You're the sum of your parts and more
You've been growing roots all along
And if those roots are truly strong
Inside of you, is where you will find home.

Festival of Lights

Festival of Lights around the corner
A to do list a mile long
But the distance to home is even longer
A reminder of where I am from
'So ambitious, you take on too much'
Is what I hear most often
But really, my busy-ness as such
Is just a way to soften
The reminder that after eons spent here
I still feel displaced, out of place, misplaced
And with every diya I light or mithai I make
I will never truly replicate
The taste of home, those sounds and smells
Of heady camphor and temple bells
My children will never know the rush
Of early morning wakings
Of frantic ladoo making
But even more important than that
The camaraderie and kinship
Of family and community
Hard to capture in an occasional trip
I've made my peace with the nostalgia
The past is literally so distant
And I work on my mile long list
Knowing how futile is my resistance

The stronger to the past my hold
The harder for new traditions to unfold.

Aesthetic

Neutrals are the new aesthetic
Crisp whites and bougie beige
Or sometimes the seasons new pick
Maybe an inoffensive sage,
Organic modern is all the rage
Timeless, natural, elemental
No bright splash of color to assail
Your deceptively expensive shade of gray,
The do's and don'ts list is long
To make your home insta worthy
Bafflingly, perpetually clean homes
That never ever seem to get dirty
Designs that feel seamless and cohesive
With non-matchy furniture blended together to
give
The look and feel of a world so striking and
dreamy,
Unattainable standards of beauty
They don't just exist for our bodies anymore
Homes that somehow look cozy and yet unlived
Are the new standards to strive for,
Karate chopped pillows and spotless floors
Bright copper kettles and warm woolen throws,
Tips on how to make your house smell like fall,
But the real question to ask is not

How to make your house look like that
It's to ask whether you want to live in a home or
TikTok
Because a home should be where you can be
yourself at.

Checklist

As soon as your nascent cries break through
The veil of this world brand new
You are handed a checklist of to do's,
Your predetermined path of fortune.

There's an order to these things -
An agenda of curated milestones,
To ensure, you're told, that you live a life most optimal,
Stay the course and follow the rules cardinal .

Why yes- you do have options
Meticulously and conveniently
Whittled down to Option A and B.
Take Option B - the road less travelled,
But you're still in the safe zone
Well within the scaffold.

Meandering isn't encouraged
But as long as you find your way back,
You will be accepted into the fold
Perhaps face the slightest flack,
But should you ever choose to forego
The checklist altogether,
Know that you wade into the choppy waters

Of uncertainty and possible regret
No options to choose or mileposts to validate
Every direction is vast overwhelming stretches
of sea
But swim in whichever way - it's a new
possibility.

Wonder

Her eyes are big with wonder
As she learns about the planets and space
And I wonder at and about that feeling of awe
And the light of curiosity furrowing her face,
What it must feel like to learn about this world
for the first time
The simplest of things seem magical,
How the car works and words rhyme
Are all a source of extreme delight.
When the garage door opens to her 'Open
Sesame' commands
Or she discovers the joy of bubbles
And the magic of kinetic sand
The unprompted shriek that a tumbling tower
incites
The giddiness of running with abandon
Or the jaw dropping moment a kite takes flight
Or learning how the earth rotates around the sun,
A humble reminder when I see the world
through her eyes
That the world truly is wonderful
And always experiencing it as if for the first
time
Is in itself the best prize.